# EXPLANATORY NOTES

CHILDREN ACT 2004

**GRAN*GIS* UK Publishing**

Adapted and published by GRANGIS (Grand Register Library).
Online: www.grangis.com
E-mail: contact@grangis.com


In this version:
ISBN: 979-8-88559-040-2

Note: This is the original version (as it was originally enacted). Title, sub-title and the generated date is as marked on the pages.

*These notes refer to the Children Act 2004 (c.31)*

---

# EXPLANATORY NOTES

## CHILDREN ACT 2004


**INTRODUCTION**

**Summary and Background**

**Territorial Application**

**COMMENTARY ON SECTIONS**

**PART 1 - CHILDREN'S COMMISSIONER**

Section 1: Establishment

Schedule 1: Children's Commissioner

Section 2: General function

Section 3: Inquiries initiated by the Commissioner

Section 4: Other inquiries held by the Commissioner

Section 5: Functions of Commissioner in Wales

Section 6: Functions of Commissioner in Scotland

Section 7: Functions of Commissioner in Northern Ireland

Section 8: Annual reports

Section 9: Care leavers and young persons with learning disabilities

**PART 2 - CHILDREN'S SERVICES IN ENGLAND**

**General**

Section 10: Co-operation to improve well-being

Section 11: Arrangements to safeguard and promote welfare

Section 12: Information databases

**Local Safeguarding Children Boards**

Section 13: Establishment of

Section 14: Functions and procedure of

Section 15: Funding of

Section 16: : supplementary

**Local authority administration**

Section 17: Children and Young People's Plans

Section 18: Director of children's services

Schedule 2: Director of children's services: consequential amendments

Section 19: Lead member for children's services

Sections 20-24: Inspections of children's services

Section 20: Joint area reviews

Section 21: Framework

Section 22: Co-operation and delegation

Section 23: Sections 20 to 22: interpretation

Section 24: Performance rating of social services

**PART 3 - CHILDREN'S SERVICES IN WALES**

**General**

Section 25: Co-operation to improve well-being: Wales

Section 26: Children and young people's plans: Wales

Section 27: Responsibility for functions under sections 25 and 26

Section 28: Arrangements to safeguard and promote welfare: Wales

Section 29: Information databases: Wales

Section 30: Inspection of functions under this Part

Sections 31-34: Local Safeguarding Children Boards: Wales

**PART 4 – ADVISORY AND SUPPORT SERVICES FOR FAMILY PROCEEDINGS**

**functions in Wales**

Section 35: Functions of the Assembly relating to family proceedings

Section 36: Ancillary powers of the Assembly

Section 37: Welsh family proceedings officers

Section 38: Inspections

Section 39: Protection of children

Section 40: Advisory and support services for family proceedings: supplementary

Schedule 3 – Advisory and support services for family proceedings

Section 41: Sharing of information

**Transfers**

Section 42: Transfer of property from to Assembly

Section 43: Transfer of staff from to Assembly

**Private fostering**

Section 44: Amendments to notification scheme

Section 45: Power to establish registration scheme in England

Section 46: Power to establish a registration scheme in Wales

Section 47: Expiry of power in sections 45 and 46

Section 48: Child minding and day care

Schedule 4: Child minding and day care

Section 49: Payments to foster parents

**Local authority services**

Section 50: Intervention

Section 51: Inspection of local education authorities

Section 52: Duty of local authorities to promote educational achievement

Section 53: Ascertaining children's wishes

Section 54: Information about individual children

Section 55: Social services committees

Schedule 5: Repeals, part 4 social services committees and departments

**Other provisions**

Section 57: Fees payable to members of independent review panel

Section 58: Reasonable punishment

Section 60: Child safety orders

Section 61: Children's Commissioner for Wales: powers of entry

Section 62: Publication of material relating to legal proceedings

Section 63: Disclosure of information by Inland Revenue

Section 67: Commencement

**Hansard References**

*These notes refer to the Children Act 2004 (c.31)*
*which received Royal Assent on 15th November 2004*

# CHILDREN ACT 2004

---

## EXPLANATORY NOTES

### INTRODUCTION

1. These explanatory notes relate to the Children Act 2004 which received Royal Assent on 15th November 2004. They have been prepared by the Department for Education and Skills (DfES) in order to assist the reader in understanding the Act. They do not form part of the Act and have not been endorsed by Parliament.

2. The notes need to be read in conjunction with the Act. They are not, and are not meant to be, a comprehensive description of the Act. So where a section or part of a section does not seem to require any explanation or comment, none is given.

### *Summary and Background*

3. In September 2003, the Government published the *Every Child Matters* Green Paper alongside its formal response to the Victoria Climbié Inquiry Report. The Green Paper proposed changes in policy and legislation in England to maximise opportunities and minimise risks for all children and young people, focusing services more effectively around the needs of children, young people and families.

4. The consultation on the Green Paper showed broad support for the proposals, in particular the intention to concentrate on outcomes that children and young people themselves have said are important, rather than prescribing organisational change. The Act has been produced in the light of this consultation and gives effect to the legislative proposals set out in the Green Paper to create clear accountability for children's services, to enable better joint working and to secure a better focus on safeguarding children. Alongside the Act, the Government has published *Every Child Matters: Next Steps*. This provides details of the consultation response and the wider, non-legislative, elements of change that are being taken forward to promote the well-being of all children.

5. To ensure a voice for children and young people at national level Part 1 of the Act provides for the establishment of a Children's Commissioner (in these notes referred to as 'the Commissioner'). Under section 2, the Commissioner's role will be to promote awareness of the views and interests of children (and certain groups of vulnerable young adults) in England. The Commissioner will also be able to hold inquiries – on direction by the Secretary of State or on his own initiative – into cases of individual children with wider policy relevance in England or, on non-devolved matters, in other parts of the UK. Sections 5, 6, and 7 give the Commissioner functions in relation to non-devolved matters in Wales, Scotland, and Northern Ireland. These functions are the same as the functions which the Commissioner has in England under sections 2, 3, and 4 namely promoting awareness of the views and interests of children and holding inquiries on direction by the Secretary of State or on his own initiative.

6. Part 2 of the Act gives effect in England to the principal legislative proposals contained in the Green Paper to support better integrated planning, commissioning, and delivery of children's services and provide for clear accountability.

7. In particular, the Act places a duty on local authorities to make arrangements through which key agencies co-operate to improve the well-being of children and young people and widen services' powers to pool budgets in support of this. To ensure that, within this partnership working, safeguarding children continues to be given priority the Act places a responsibility for key agencies to have regard to the need to safeguard children and promote their welfare in exercising their normal functions. It also establishes statutory Local Safeguarding Children Boards to replace the existing non-statutory Area Child Protection Committees. In addition, it provides for regulations to require children's services authorities to prepare and publish a Children and Young People's Plan (CYPP) which will set out their strategy for services for children and relevant young people (sections 10, 11, 13-16, 17).

8. To support professionals in working together and sharing information to identify difficulties and provide appropriate support, this part of the Act also allows for the creation of databases holding information on all children and young people (section 12).

9. Part 2 includes measures to ensure clear accountability for children's services. The Act will require local authorities in England to put in place a director of children's services to be accountable for, as a minimum, the local authority's education and social services functions in so far as they relate to children. It will also require the designation of a lead member for children's services to mirror the director's responsibilities at a local political level (sections 18 and 19).

10. To ensure a shared approach across inspections, sections 20 to 24 allow for the creation of an integrated inspection framework and for inspectorates to carry out joint reviews of all children's services provided in an area. (In support of this integrated approach, section 50 extends existing intervention powers in relation to education functions of local authorities to children's social services.)

11. Part 3 of the Act provides for similar provisions to those in Part 2 to be made in Wales, but allows for implementation within the different context that exists for children's services there. In particular, reflecting this difference, in Wales authorities will be required to identify lead directors and members for children's services for local authorities, local health boards and NHS trusts. For Wales there are no provisions on inspection equivalent to those in sections 20 to 24.

12. Part 4 of the Act provides for the devolution of CAFCASS functions in Wales to the Assembly.

13. Part 5 of the Act makes a number of further provisions:

- to strengthen the existing notification arrangements for private fostering, with a reserve power to introduce a registration scheme should these not prove effective (sections 44 to 47);
- to clarify and simplify the registration of child minders and providers of day care (section 48);
- to make provision for the level of payments to be made to foster parents caring for looked after children placed with them by local authorities and to foster parents caring for children placed with them by voluntary organisations (section 49);
- to provide for the extension of existing intervention powers as mentioned above (section 50);
- to provide for an extension of inspection powers under section 38 of the Education Act 1997 (section 51);
- to create a new duty for local authorities to promote the educational achievement of looked after children and an associated power to transmit data relating to individual children in monitoring this (section 52 and 54);

- to place on local authorities a new duty, before determining what (if any) services to provide under section 17 of the Children Act 1989 for a particular child in need, to ascertain the child's wishes and feelings regarding the provision of those services, and give due consideration to them (section 53);
- to remove now unnecessary provisions in relation to social services committees (section 55);
- to allow for the payment of fees to adoption review panel members (section 57);
- to restrict the grounds on which the battery of a child may be justified as reasonable punishment (section 58);
- to allow grants to be paid across the range of children, young people and families services (section 59);
- to remove the power to make a care order at a lower threshold than would be usual under the Children Act 1989 as a sanction for not complying with a Child Safety Order (section 60);
- to give the Children's Commissioner for Wales the power to enter premises, other than private homes, to interview children when reviewing and monitoring the functions of and arrangements made by the Assembly and other specified persons (section 61);
- to amend section 97 of the Children Act 1989 and section 12 of the Administration of Justice Act 1960 to make clear that the publication of material from family proceedings which is intended, or likely, to identify any child as being involved in such proceedings (or the address or school of such a child) is only prohibited in relation to publication of information to the public or any section of the public and make it clear that rules of court will set out the cases in which publication of information relating to children is authorised (section 62);
- to amend Schedule 5 of the Tax Credits Act 2002 to enable the Inland Revenue to share Tax Credit, Child Benefit or Guardian's Allowance information (except where it relates to a person's income) with local authorities (or, in Northern Ireland, Health and Social Services Boards) for the purposes of enquiries and investigations relating to the welfare of a child (section 63).

### *Territorial Application*

14. Part 1 of the Act, which establishes the Commissioner, extends to the whole of the United Kingdom.

15. Part 2 is concerned only with England and Part 3 only with Wales. Part 4 devolves to Wales functions previously exercised across England and Wales together. The provisions of Part 5 on the whole apply to England and Wales together (although sections 45 and 46 provide separate powers for registration schemes in England and Wales respectively). Section 63 applies to the whole of the UK.

## COMMENTARY ON SECTIONS

### Part 1 - Children's Commissioner

#### *Section 1: Establishment*

16. *Subsection (1)* establishes the office of the Commissioner. *Subsection (2)* gives effect to Schedule 1.

### *Schedule 1*: ***Children's Commissioner***

17. This Schedule makes provision concerning the status, general powers, appointment, and remuneration of the Commissioner. It provides for the staffing of his office, and accounting procedures. It also adds the Commissioner and members of his staff to the list of office holders who are disqualified from being members of the House of Commons or the Northern Ireland Assembly.

18. *Paragraph 3(2)* of Schedule 1 places a duty on the Secretary of State to involve children in the appointment of the Commissioner to the extent he feels is appropriate and in a manner he chooses.

19. *Paragraph 11* of Schedule 1 amends the Criminal Justice and Court Services Act 2000. Section 35 of the Act makes it an offence for someone who is disqualified under the Act from working with children knowingly to apply for, offer to do, accept or do any work in a regulated position as defined in section 36. *Paragraph 11* adds the Commissioner and his deputy to the list of regulated positions in section 36.

### *Section 2*: ***General function***

20. The general function of the Commissioner is set out in *subsection (1)*. The Commissioner is to promote awareness of the views and interests of children in England. As well as those under 18, the term 'children' includes persons aged 18, 19 and 20 who have been looked after by a local authority at any time after attaining the age of 16 or who have a learning disability. He will be expected to raise the profile of the issues that affect and concern children in England, and promote awareness and understanding of their views and interests among all sectors of society, both public and private. The Commissioner will therefore be expected actively to gather and understand the views of children from all backgrounds. However, the Commissioner will also be expected to use his own judgement in determining the interests of children, which may not always be the same as their own expressed wishes, especially with younger children.

21. *Subsection (2)* provides more detail of what the Commissioner may do in the exercise of his function. The Commissioner, under *subsection (2)(a)*, may encourage persons exercising functions or engaged in activities affecting children, to take account of their views and interests. In exercising that power, it is intended that he will encourage them, for example by sharing best practice, to ensure that the views and interests of children inform the development and delivery of their policies and practices. Not only will the Commissioner want to represent the views of children, he will encourage such persons to be proactive in gathering children's views themselves.

22. Under *subsection (2)(b)* the Commissioner is to be able to give advice to the relevant Secretary of State on matters affecting children, such as the development of policy or legislation. It is intended that the Commissioner will give advice on his own initiative and respond to requests for advice from any Secretary of State, but due to constraints on time and resources this may not always be possible, and the Commissioner will be expected to use his own judgment to prioritise requests.

23. In considering or researching the operation of complaints procedures under *subsection (2)(c)* the Commissioner will want to see that they are effective and quick and easy for children to access and follow. The Commissioner will be able to look at any services, procedures or arrangements relevant to children, both public and private. It is envisaged that in doing this the Commissioner will work with the relevant Ombudsmen and statutory bodies as appropriate.

24. Under *subsection (2)(d)* the Commissioner will have wide discretion over other matters relating to the interests of children that he chooses to consider or research.

25. Under *subsection (2)(e)* the Commissioner will be able to publish a report on any matter considered or researched by him while carrying out his section 2 function.

26. In carrying out his general function the Commissioner should have particular regard to the aspects of well-being set out in *subsection (3)(a) – (e)*. These reflect the five outcomes which, during the development of the Green Paper *Every Child Matters*, children identified as being the most important to them. It is intended that they form the framework for the Commissioner's activities. Through carrying out his general function the Commissioner will monitor and stimulate progress towards achieving these outcomes for all children.

27. *Subsection (4)* places a duty on the Commissioner to take reasonable steps to involve children in all of his work. This will ensure that his work is informed by the views of children. In particular the Commissioner has to make sure that children know what he does and how to contact him. He must also consult children and organisations which work with them on the work to be undertaken by him. It will be for the Commissioner to determine how he does this as is appropriate to the circumstances. The intention is that the views of children drive the work of the Commissioner.

28. *Subsection (5)* requires the Commissioner, when publishing a report made under this section, to publish the report in a version that is suitable for children or a particular group of children, as the Commissioner feels is appropriate.

29. The intention behind *subsection (6)* is that the Commissioner should pay particular regard to disadvantaged children who are most vulnerable or may need extra support in making their views known. It is intended that the Commissioner will be proactive in seeking and reflecting the views of children whose voices might not otherwise be listened to.

30. *Subsection (7)* prohibits the Commissioner from conducting investigations into individual cases. The intention is that this will allow him to concentrate on the broader issues that affect children.

31. *Subsection (8)* is intended to ensure that the Commissioner can get access to children for the purpose of getting their views. It ensures that the Commissioner can access children accommodated or cared for outside their homes (for example, in young offender institutions, children's homes or residential schools) and gives him access to such establishments and the right to speak to a child in private if the child consents to this.

32. To assist the Commissioner further, *subsection (9)* places a duty upon bodies with statutory functions to provide him with information that he requests as long as it is information that they already hold and can be disclosed lawfully to the Commissioner.

33. *Subsection (10)* gives the Commissioner the power to follow up recommendations made by him in any of the reports he produces when carrying out his duties under section 2. Bodies with statutory functions that are subject to recommendations must inform the Commissioner, in writing, in any time period dictated by the Commissioner, what action they are taking or proposing to take in response to these recommendations.

34. Under *subsections (11)* and *(12)* the Commissioner must have regard to the relevant provisions of the United Nations Convention on the Rights of the Child (UNCRC) in his consideration of what the interests of children are. The Commissioner's work will be driven and shaped by the views and interests of children. The UNCRC provides a set of principles to which the Commissioner may wish to refer and upon which he may wish to draw as he carries out his function.

### *Section 3: Inquiries initiated by the Commissioner*

35. This section permits the Commissioner to initiate inquiries into individual cases that meet certain criteria. It applies to all matters relating to children in England.

36. *Subsections (1) and (2)* set out the criteria that the Commissioner must consider before starting an inquiry. The case concerned must raise issues of public policy that would be relevant to other children. This would for example mean that the Commissioner could

hold an inquiry into the case of a child in a children's home or a residential school if the issues involved were relevant in general to children in such an establishment, but not if they were only relevant to children in that particular establishment. The Commissioner must satisfy himself that an inquiry would not duplicate the work that was the function of another person and to this end he must consult others who might have such a function. The Commissioner could carry out an inquiry if after conducting the appropriate consultation he had established that a person who might carry out an inquiry was not going to do so; or that his inquiry would be looking at an aspect of a case which was different from the aspect that someone else's inquiry would look at so his inquiry would not amount to a duplication of work. The aim of the inquiry must be to investigate the public policy issues arising from the case and make recommendations relating to them.

37. *Subsection (3)* requires the Commissioner to consult the Secretary of State before holding an inquiry. The Secretary of State may offer guidance, but has no power to veto an inquiry: the final decision is for the Commissioner. *Sub-section (4)* allows the Commissioner to decide whether to hold all or part of an inquiry in private.

38. *Subsection (5)* requires the Commissioner to publish a report and send a copy of it to the Secretary of State as soon as possible after completing the report. S*ubsection (6)* permits the Commissioner to protect a child's identity in the inquiry report.

39. *Subsection (7)* gives the Commissioner the power to follow up recommendations made by him in any report he produces after conducting an inquiry that he himself has initiated. Bodies with statutory functions that are subject to recommendations must inform the Commissioner, in writing, in any time period dictated by the Commissioner, what action they are taking or proposing to take in response to these recommendations.

40. *Subsection (8)* gives the Commissioner a range of powers to assist him in carrying out an inquiry under this section. By virtue of the application of subsections (2) and (3) of section 250 of the Local Government Act 1972 the Commissioner will, when conducting an inquiry in England, be able to summons people to attend to give evidence or to produce documents and to administer oaths and take evidence on oath and it will be an offence to disobey a summons by for example refusing to give evidence or by tampering with documentary evidence.

### *Section 4: **Other inquiries held by the Commissioner***

41. *Subsection (1)* enables the Secretary of State to direct the Commissioner to hold an inquiry into the case of an individual child, where the Secretary of State considers the case to be of wider relevance or have implications for other children. In contrast to the power under section 3, the Commissioner could under this section carry out an inquiry into a case which only has implications for a small group of children. So, for example, he could hold an inquiry into the case of a child in a children's home or a residential school if the issues involved were relevant in general to children in such an establishment, or if they were only relevant to children in that particular establishment. It is envisaged that the Commissioner will play a role in determining whether a case is relevant, for example through his ability to offer advice to the Secretary of State.

42. The Commissioner may hold the inquiry in private *(subsection (2))* and he must make and send to the Secretary of State a report in relation to the inquiry as soon as possible after he has completed it *(subsection (3))*.

43. *Subsection (4)* requires that in most cases the Secretary of State publish the report as soon as possible. Under *subsection (5),* however, where he thinks it would be undesirable for the identity of the child to be made public, he may publish an edited version of the report (making only those amendments necessary to protect the identity of the child), or, if it is not possible to publish a version of the report without identifying the child, withhold publication altogether. *Subsection (6)* requires the Secretary of State to lay a copy of each report published by him before each House of Parliament.

44. *Subsection (7)* gives the Commissioner a range of powers to assist him in carrying out an inquiry under this section. By virtue of the application of subsections (2) to (5) of section 250 of the Local Government Act 1972 the Commissioner will, when conducting an inquiry in England, be able to summons people to attend to give evidence or to produce documents and to administer oaths and take evidence on oath; it will be an offence to disobey a summons by for example refusing to give evidence or by tampering with documentary evidence; the Secretary of State can direct parties to the inquiry to pay his costs and make orders for parties to pay the costs of other parties to the inquiry.

### *Section 5: **Functions of Commissioner in Wales***

45. *Subsection (1)* gives the Commissioner the function of promoting awareness of the views and interests of children in Wales, but only in relation to those matters which do not already fall within the remit of the Children's Commissioner for Wales under section 72B, 73 or 74 of the Care Standards Act 2000. The functions given to the Children's Commissioner for Wales by those sections (the review of the exercise of functions of the Assembly and other specified bodies, the review and monitoring of various arrangements made by specified bodies, and the examination of particular cases) extend to bodies that have statutory functions in Wales or that provide statutory services that come within the functions of the Assembly. *Subsection (2)* gives the Commissioner the same powers and duties in relation to this function as he has for his function under section 2.

46. *Subsection (3)* places a duty on the Commissioner to take account of the views of and any work undertaken by the Children's Commissioner for Wales when he is carrying out his function under subsection (1).

47. *Subsections (4) and (6)* give to the Commissioner the power to undertake inquiries, at his own initiation and at the direction of the Secretary of State respectively, in relation to the case of an individual child in Wales, so long as it does not fall within the remit of the Children's Commissioner for Wales as described in subsection (1). *Subsections (5) and (7)* import to those inquiry functions the powers and duties given to the Commissioner in respect of inquiries carried out under sections 3 and 4.

### *Section 6: **Functions of Commissioner in Scotland***

48. *Subsection (1)* gives the Commissioner the function of promoting awareness of the views and interests of children in Scotland in relation to reserved matters. *Subsection (2)* gives the Commissioner the same powers and duties in relation to this function as he has for his function under section 2.

49. *Subsection (3)* places a duty on the Commissioner to take account of the views of, and any work undertaken by, the Commissioner for Children and Young People in Scotland when he is carrying out his function outlined in subsection (1).

50. *Subsections (4) and (7)* give to the Commissioner the power to undertake inquiries, at his own initiation and at the direction of the Secretary of State respectively, in relation to the case of an individual child in Scotland so long as the issues raised by it relate to a reserved matter.

### *Section 7: **Functions of Commissioner in Northern Ireland***

51. *Subsection (1)* gives the Commissioner the function of promoting awareness of the views and interests of children in Northern Ireland in relation to excepted matters. *Subsection (2)* gives the Commissioner the same powers and duties in relation to this function as he has for his function under section 2.

52. *Subsection (3)* places a duty on the Commissioner to take account of the views of, and any work undertaken by, the Commissioner for Children and Young People for Northern Ireland when he is carrying out his function outlined in subsection (1).

53. *Subsections (4) and (7)* give to the Commissioner the power to undertake inquiries, at his own initiation and at the direction of the Secretary of State respectively, in relation to the case of an individual child in Northern Ireland so long as the issues raised by it relate to an excepted matter.

### *Section 8: Annual reports*

54. *Subsection (1)* requires the Commissioner to report annually on what he has done, what he has found and what he intends to consider or research in the coming year.

55. The Commissioner will send his annual report to the Secretary of State who must lay the report, unchanged, and as soon as possible, before both Houses of Parliament. The Commissioner will be responsible for publishing, publicising and disseminating the report.

56. The Commissioner must as he thinks appropriate produce a child-friendly version of his annual report.

### *Section 9: Care leavers and young persons with learning disabilities*

57. This section extends the definition of children in relation to all the Commissioner's functions. As well as those under 18, it is to include persons aged 18, 19 and 20 who have been looked after by a local authority at any time after attaining the age of 16 or who have a learning disability.

58. *Subsection (3)* defines 'looked after by a local authority' and 'learning disability'.

59. In the exercise of his functions under Part 1 therefore the Commissioner is to be concerned with all people under the age of 18 and those over 18 but under 21 who come within one of the two specified groups. However, the extension of the definition of children does not apply for the purposes of section 2(11) and 2(12) so that the Commissioner only has to have regard to the United Nations Convention on the Rights of the Child when he is determining what constitutes the interests of those under the age of 18.

## Part 2 - Children's Services in England

## General

### *Section 10: Co-operation to improve well-being*

60. The purpose of this section is to create a statutory framework for local co-operation between local authorities, key partner agencies ('relevant partners') and other relevant bodies ('other bodies or persons'), including the voluntary and community sector, in order to improve the well-being of children in the area. The duty to make these arrangements is placed on the local authority and a duty to co-operate with the local authority is placed on the relevant partners. As well as underpinning wide co-operation arrangements, these duties and powers will also provide the statutory context within which agencies will be encouraged to integrate commissioning and delivery of children's services, underpinned by pooled budgeting arrangements, in Children's Trusts.

61. *Subsection (1)* imposes a duty on the local authority to make arrangements to promote co-operation between the authority, its relevant partners (listed in *subsection (4))* and other bodies exercising functions or engaged in activities relating to children in the authority's area. The duty on each partner agency to co-operate is in *subsection (5). Subsection (4)(f)* refers to the Connexions Service.

62. *Subsection (2)* sets out the purposes of such arrangements. They are to be made with a view to improving the well-being of children in the authority's area. This subsection also specifies the aspects of well-being with which such arrangements are concerned.

These reflect the five outcomes which children identified as being most important to them.

63. *Subsection (3)* ensures that in making arrangements, children's services authorities must have regard to the importance of the role of parents and carers in improving the well-being of children.

64. *Subsections (6)* and *(7)* give a power for all the specified partners to provide staff, goods, services, accommodation or other resources and to pool budgets in support of these arrangements.

65. *Subsection (8)* requires those subject to the duties to have regard to guidance from the Secretary of State. This guidance will be issued jointly by the relevant government departments to all of the relevant partners. It is likely that the guidance will set out the outcomes expected of these arrangements. These include: effective working together to understand the needs of local children, agreeing the contribution each agency should make to meet those needs, effective sharing of information at a strategic level and about individual children to support multi-agency working, and oversight of arrangements for agencies to work together in integrated planning, commissioning and delivery of services as appropriate. The guidance will, in particular, make clear that, for the local authority and Primary Care Trust and other participating services (e.g. Connexions, Youth Offending Teams) these arrangements should include consideration of integrated commissioning in the delivery of children's services. There will also be guidance as to the kinds of other bodies and persons referred to in *subsection (1)(c)* which the local authority may involve in these arrangements.

66. *Subsection (9)* permits arrangements made under this section to include those relating to persons aged 18 and 19 and persons over 19 receiving services as care leavers under the Children Act 1989 and persons under 25 with learning difficulties receiving services under the Learning and Skills Act 2000.

### *Section 11: **Arrangements to safeguard and promote welfare***

67. This section imposes a duty on specified agencies to make arrangements to ensure that their functions are discharged having regard to the need to safeguard and promote the welfare of children. The aim of this duty is to:

- complement the general co-operation duty (section 10) in the specific area of children's safeguards;
- ensure that agencies give appropriate priority to their responsibilities towards the children in their care or with whom they come into contact;
- encourage agencies to share early concerns about safety and welfare of children and to ensure preventative action before a crisis develops.

68. This duty is intended to ensure that agencies are conscious of the need to safeguard children and promote their welfare in the course of executing their normal functions. Exercise of this duty will require agencies that come into contact with children to recognise that their needs are not always the same as adults i.e. that they are children, and vulnerable, as well as being patients, offenders, or people who use local amenities.

- *Subsection (1)* sets out the persons and bodies to which the duty applies.
- *Subsection (2)* sets out the duty and makes clear that it continues to apply where the relevant body contracts out services.
- *Subsection (3)* excludes the application of the duty where section 175 of the Education Act 2002 applies. That section places a similar duty on Local Education Authorities, schools and further education colleges, i.e. to make arrangements for ensuring that their functions are exercised with a view to safeguarding and

promoting the welfare of children and to have regard to guidance issued for this purpose by the Secretary of State.

- *Subsection (4)* requires those exercising the duty to have regard to guidance from the Secretary of State.

### *Section 12: Information databases*

69. This section creates a power for the Secretary of State by regulations made by affirmative resolution procedure (section 66(3) refers) to require local authorities to establish and operate a database or databases of information about all children and other young people to whom arrangements under section 10 or 11 or section 175 of the Education Act 2002 may relate *(subsection (1)(a))*. Alternatively, the Secretary of State may set up such databases himself and he may set up a body corporate to operate such databases *(subsections (1)(b) and (2))*. Such databases might be set up at a local, regional or national level.

70. The purpose of the information databases that would be set up under this section is to facilitate contact between professionals who are supporting individual children or who have concerns about their development, well-being or welfare with the aim of securing early, coherent, intervention. The purpose of including the basic data set out in *subsection (4)* is to help practitioners identify quickly a child they have contact with, and whether that child is getting the universal services (education, primary health care) to which he or she is entitled. Such data, suitably anonymised, would also serve a purpose in service planning. These purposes relate directly to the overarching duties on service providers to co-operate to promote the well-being of children (section 10) and to safeguard and promote the welfare of children (section 11). The purposes for which information databases may be used also include the duty of Local Education Authorities and governing bodies to fulfil their functions in a way that safeguards and promotes the welfare of children under section 175 of the Education Act 2002.

71. The section sets out the principles that would govern information sharing using information databases, including the basic information that is to be included in respect of all children. The detailed operational requirements will be set out in the affirmative procedure regulations referred to above and, as to more technical matters, in directions and guidance issued by the Secretary of State under *subsections (12) and (13)*.

72. *Subsection (3)* provides that a database may only include information specified in subsection (4) in relation to a person to whom subsection (1) relates (i.e. all children and other young people within the scope of sections 10 and 11 and section 175 of the Education Act 2002).

73. *Subsection (4)* describes the information to be held on the database. The basic data to be held for all children comprises: name; address; gender; date of birth; a unique identifying number; name and contact details of any person with parental responsibility or who has day to day care of the child; details of any education being received whether in an educational institution or other setting; name and contact details of a GP practice. The subsection also provides for the inclusion of the name and contact details of any practitioner providing a specialist service (of a kind to be specified in the regulations) to a child and the fact that a practitioner has a concern about a child. No material relating to case notes or case history about an individual may be included on the database, but the flexibility exists to require the inclusion of further basic data, for example to provide for future organisational change.

74. *Subsection (5)* gives the Secretary of State power to make provision for the establishment and operation of information sharing databases.

75. *Subsection (6)* lists a number of matters concerning the management and operation of information databases that may, in particular, be included in the regulations made under *subsection (5)*. These include requiring or permitting specified types of people

or bodies to disclose information to the database, the conditions under which agencies and individuals will be granted access, the length of time that information should be held on the database and procedures for ensuring the accuracy of the data.

76. *Subsection (7)* lists the people and bodies who can be required to disclose information for inclusion in the database. This enables the primary sources of the basic data to be Primary Care Trusts, Local Education Authorities and the Connexions Service, with other statutory bodies and registered independent schools having a duty to supply such other information as may be required.

77. *Subsection (8)* lists the people and bodies who can be permitted to disclose information for inclusion in the database. This provides for voluntary sector bodies and the Inland Revenue (for Child Benefit and Child Tax Credit records), among others, to respond to any requests by the people who may be required to establish the databases to fill in any gaps in the basic data.

78. *Subsection (9)* permits information held by government departments, such as benefit records from the Department for Work and Pensions, to be supplied on request to fill in gaps in the basic data.

79. *Subsection (10)* allows the regulations to provide for the delegation of decisions relating to the matters referred to in *subsection (6)(e)*, relating to access to the databases, to persons who may be required to establish the databases.

80. *Subsection (11)* allows the regulations to provide that people or bodies who are permitted under *subsections (6)(c) to (e) or (9)* to disclose information to the database may do so notwithstanding their common law duty of confidence. Such a power would be relied upon where practitioners believe, in their professional judgement, that it is in the best interest of the child to share information about that child.

81. *Subsection (12)* provides that any direction issued by the Secretary of State must be complied with by any person or body who establishes or operates a database under this section and that they must have regard to any guidance issued by the Secretary of State.

82. *Subsection (13)* lists matters concerning the operation of the information databases that may, in particular, be included in directions or guidance issued by the Secretary of State. These include management functions, technical specifications, conditions relating to database security, the transfer and cross-matching of information from one database to another and the issuing of advice to children and their parents about their rights, under the Data Protection Act 1998, to access information held about them on the database.

## Local Safeguarding Children Boards

### *Section 13: **Establishment of LSCBs***

83. The purpose of this section is to place local arrangements for co-ordinating the work of key agencies in relation to safeguarding children on a statutory footing.

84. *Subsection (1)* requires each local authority to establish a Local Safeguarding Children Board (LSCB). The agencies which are 'Board partners' are listed in *subsection (3)*. The authority must co-operate with the Board partners in establishing the Board and the Board partners each have a reciprocal obligation to co-operate with the local authority *(subsection (7))*.

85. *Subsection (2)* provides for the Secretary of State to make regulations about representation on the LSCB. For example, regulations might be used to ensure that every Board partner, and the local authority, had a representative on the LSCB, albeit possibly through two or more sharing a single representative. Regulations may also set out the level of seniority required of representatives.

86. *Subsections (4)* and *(5)* provide for representation from persons other than Board partners exercising functions or engaged in activities in relation to children in the area. These might include schools and voluntary groups. The local authority must take steps to ensure representation of prescribed persons (*subsection (4)*) and may also invite representation from other persons or groups in consultation with Board partners (*subsection (5)*). This reflects that there will be other bodies in each area with a contribution to make to the work of the LSCB. It also allows the Board to seek specialist expertise where it sees fit.

87. *Subsection (8)* enables two or more local authorities to join together to establish an LSCB covering their combined areas.

### *Section 14: **Functions and procedure of LSCBs***

88. *Subsection (1)* sets out the objective of LSCBs. The aim is to ensure that each local area has a coherent approach to safeguarding children based on contributions from all key agencies, and that this approach is managed effectively.

89. *Subsection (2)* allows for functions of LSCBs to be prescribed by the Secretary of State in regulations. These functions will largely be based on the functions of their predecessor bodies, Area Child Protection Committees, as set out in Government guidance *Working Together to Safeguard Children* and will support the overall objective of the Board.

90. *Subsection (3)* allows for the Secretary of State to prescribe the procedures to be followed by LSCBs. For example, it may require a register of attendance to be kept.

### *Section 15: **Funding of LSCBs***

91. This section enables the local authority and the Board partners to contribute financially to the cost of establishing and running the LSCB. It allows for money from those agencies to be pooled in a single fund. It also makes clear that partners can provide non-pecuniary resources (such as staff, goods, services or accommodation) in support of the activities of the LSCB.

92. Where the governor or director of prison service institution or secure training centre is a Board partner the power to contribute is given to the Secretary of State. Where the prison or secure training centre is contracted out, the power to contribute is given to the contractor.

### *Section 16: **LSCBs: supplementary***

93. *Subsection (1)* enables regulations to provide for the functions of local authorities in relation to LSCBs. These will cover such matters as provision of administrative and support services.

94. *Subsection (2)* provides that, in exercising their functions, the authority and its Board partners must have regard to any guidance issued by the Secretary of State for this purpose. This guidance may, for example, set out how contributions may be made in cash or kind and how arrangements should be made for investigation of unexpected child deaths, and provide further detail about the functions and management of LSCBs.

## Local authority administration

### *Section 17: **Children and Young People's Plans***

95. Section 17 imposes a new duty on children's services authorities to plan for the provision of services for children. It is linked to the duty to co-operate which is the subject of section 10. As a consequence of the new duty, a number of other planning obligations falling on local authorities are being dispensed with. These are the Education Development Plan, the Early Years Development and Childcare Plan,

the School Organisation Plan, the Behaviour Support Plan, the Class Sizes Plan, the Children's Services Plan and the Local Authority Adoption Services Plan.

96. *Subsection (1)* provides for regulations to require children's services authorities to prepare and publish a Children and Young People's Plan (CYPP) which will set out their strategy for services for children and relevant young people.

97. *Subsection (2)* states that regulations may make provision for the content, timescale, publication and review of the plan and what consultation should be undertaken in its preparation. We intend the CYPP to be based on the five outcomes for children and to contain a statement of local vision for children and young people, key outcomes, a strategic analysis, actions (with timescales), references to joint planning with key partners, performance management and review of children's services, and to outline the consultation undertaken in its preparation. The intention is that regulations will provide for the CYPP to relate to successive periods of three years. The authority will have to publish the CYPP and to review it annually.

98. *Subsection (3)* provides for the content of the plan to include arrangements made under section 10 (duty to co-operate) and the strategy of key partners with whom there is co-operation for children's services. Therefore, the CYPP will be consistent with plans for services for children and young people prepared by other organisations in respect of the local authority's area, e.g. concerning children's health services, youth justice and services provided by the voluntary and community sector.

99. Relevant young people are defined according to section 10(9).

### *Section 18: **Director of children's services***

100. The local authorities that are children's services authorities for the purposes of this Act are currently required to appoint a chief education officer and a director of social services. Those requirements are removed when authorities exercise their power under this section to appoint a director of children's services and a director of adult social services. The Act makes it possible for local authorities to make these appointments and gives the Secretary of State a power to require them to do so by order at such time as he thinks appropriate.

101. The purposes for which the director of children's services is appointed are local authority education functions (other than functions specified in relation to adults); social services functions for children; functions in relation to young persons leaving care; functions conferred on the authority under sections 10- 12 and 17 of this Act; any functions delegated to the authority by an NHS body under section 31 of the Health Act 1999, so far as relating to children; and any other function prescribed by the Secretary of State by regulations. The authority may include in the remit of the director of children's services such additional functions as they consider appropriate *(subsection (5))*. Authorities are free, for example, to include adult education functions.

102. Directors of children's services will also be expected to steer local co-operation arrangements in relation to children's services. Further detail on the role and responsibilities of the director will be set out in guidance issued by the Secretary of State under *subsection (7)*.

103. *Subsection (8)* allows two or more authorities to appoint jointly a director of children's services. This would, for example allow adjoining authorities to reinforce arrangements for joint services.

104. *Subsection (9)* gives effect to Schedule 2.

### *Schedule 2: **Director of children's services: consequential amendments***

105. The amendments in this Schedule remove the duties for authorities in England to appoint a director of social services and a chief education officer (*paragraphs 2(2)(a)*

and *4(2)* respectively). Their functions are assigned instead to the director of children's services appointed under section 18 and the director of adult social services appointed under section 6 of the Local Authority Social Services Act 1970, as amended. Other amendments in the Schedule reflect these changes.

106. *Paragraph 1:* Section 96 of the Children and Young Persons Act 1933 (c.12) is amended to add a reference to the director of children's services. This will allow a local authority or committee by resolution to empower the director of children's services, chief education officer ('CEO') in Wales or clerk to exercise powers of the authority or committee in any case which appears to him to be urgent.

107. *Paragraph 2*: Section 6 of the Local Authority Social Services Act 1970 (c.42) is amended so that a local authority in England to which the Act applies is required to appoint a director of adult social services. This is because responsibility for children's social services comes under the Director of Children's Services so an overall Director of social services is no longer appropriate. Schedule 1 to the 1970 Act (list of social service functions of local authorities) is amended so that the appointment of the director of adult social services is a social services function on which guidance may be issued under section 7 of the Act.

108. *Paragraph 3*: Section 2 of the Local Government and Housing Act 1989 (c.42) (politically restricted posts) is amended in relation to England so the posts of director of children's services and director of adult social services are 'statutory chief officer' posts and therefore 'politically restricted'. Section 1 of that Act describes the restrictions on such persons, the main one being that such a person is disqualified from being a member of the local authority.

109. *Paragraph 4:* Section 532 of the Education Act 1996 (c.56) (appointment of chief education officer) is amended to require only local education authorities in Wales to appoint a CEO.

110. Section 566 (evidence: documents) of the Education Act 1996 is amended so that a document issued by a local education authority signed by the director of children's services (in the case of an authority in England) is treated as the document it purports to be and signed by the person by whom it purports to be signed, unless the contrary is proved. This provision still applies to the CEO of an authority in Wales.

111. *Paragraph 5:* Section 8 of the Crime and Disorder Act 1998 (c.37) (parenting orders) is amended so that someone nominated by the director of children's services is a 'responsible officer' for the purposes of that section and section 9. Responsible officers have the power to make applications to the court in respect of parenting orders and can direct a person subject to such an order to attend counselling or guidance sessions.

112. Section 39 of the Crime and Disorder Act 1998 (youth offending teams) is amended to include at least one person with experience of social work, and at least one person with experience in education to be nominated by the director of children's services on the list of persons one of who must be on every youth offending team.

113. *Paragraph 6:* Section 4C of the Protection of Children Act 1999 (c.14) is amended to substitute 'director of children's services of a local authority in England or a director of social services of a local authority in Wales' for 'director of social services of a local authority'. These post-holders are among the people who are able to apply to the High Court for an order restoring an individual's name to the list of those considered unsuitable to work with children, where it is necessary in order to protect children.

114. *Paragraph 7:* Section 36 of the Criminal Justice and Court Services Act 2000 (c.43) is amended so that the director of children's services and director of adult social services are added as a 'regulated position' for the purposes of that Act. As a consequence, under Part 2 of that Act (protection of children) a person disqualified from working with children commits an offence is he applies for the position of director of children's services.

115. *Paragraph 8:* Section 322 of the Criminal Justice Act 2003 (c.44) (individual support orders) is amended to include, in the new section 1AA (10) of the Crime and Disorder Act 1998 being inserted by that section, a reference to a person nominated by the director of children's services, so that person is a 'responsible officer' for the purposes of that section and section 1AB (which relate to individual support orders).

### *Section 19: **Lead member for children's services***

116. *Subsection (1)(a)* requires a local authority in England to designate one of their members as lead member for children's services in respect of the functions of the authority set out in section 18(1). *Subsection (1)(b)* allows individual authorities to allocate to the lead member for children's services any additional functions they consider appropriate.

117. Further detail on which member should be designated as the lead member (depending on individual authorities' constitutional arrangements), and the role and responsibilities of the lead member will be set out in guidance issued by the Secretary of State under *subsection (2)*.

### *Sections 20-24: **Inspections of children's services***

118. The purpose of these sections is to provide for a unified approach to the inspection of children's services in a local authority area.

### *Section 20: **Joint area reviews***

119. The purpose of this section is to make provision for joint area reviews of children's services (as defined in section 23(3)) to be carried out in the area of each children's services authority or the areas of particular children's services authorities.

120. *Subsection (1)* provides that the Secretary of State can request the inspectorates and commissions to draw up a timetable for joint area reviews for his approval. *Subsection (1)(a)(i)* allows the request to include every children's services authority, depending which authority is being reviewed; *subsection (1)(a)(ii)* allows the request to cover some but not all of the children's services authorities. *Subsection (1)(b)* enables the Secretary of State to request two or more of the inspectorates to conduct a review of particular children's services in an area he specifies. Where the Secretary of State makes such a request the inspectorates in question are obliged to conduct the review.

121. *Subsection (2)* enables two or more of the inspectorates to conduct a review of a particular local authority's area on their own initiative.

122. *Subsection (3)* provides that the purpose of the review is to evaluate the extent to which, taken together, the children's services being reviewed improve the well-being of children and relevant young persons. The review will, in particular, consider the quality of children's services and how the bodies which provide those services work together.

123. *Subsections (5) and (6)* provides that any review must be conducted in accordance with arrangements made by Her Majesty's Chief Inspector of Schools ('Chief Inspector') and before making those arrangements he must consult the inspectorates as he considers appropriate.

124. *Subsection (7)* provides that the Chief Inspector's annual report under section 2 (7)(a) of the School Inspections Act 1996 must include an account of reviews carried out under this section.

125. *Subsection (8)* enables the Secretary of State to make regulations in relation to reviews under this section. This may include making provision to require the persons or bodies inspected to produce information for the purposes of a review, or to authorise entry to premises for those conducting reviews and provision creating criminal offences to underpin these obligations. By virtue of *subsections (9) and (10)* provision can be made

by applying existing provisions giving the inspectorates powers to conduct assessments for the purpose of reviews under section 20. 'Assessment' for the purposes of the section is defined in section 23(2) (see below). Regulations may also impose requirements as to the making of a report on each review under this section and for specified persons to make written statements of the action they propose to take in light of the report and the period within which such action must or may be taken.

### *Section 21: Framework*

126. This section makes provision for a Framework for Inspection of Children's Services ('the Framework').

127. *Subsection (1)* imposes a duty on the Chief Inspector of Schools to devise the Framework. The purpose of the Framework is to set out the principles which are to be applied by any of the inspectorates when carrying out a relevant assessment (see section 23 (2)) of children's services, including a joint area review under section 20. The purpose of the Framework is to ensure that those assessments properly evaluate and report on the extent to which children's services improve the well-being of children and relevant young persons. The principles may include how the results of an assessment are to be organised and reported by each of the inspectorates, so that their judgement 'ratings' may be aggregated.

128. *Subsection (6)* provides that the Chief Inspector must consult the inspectorates when devising the Framework. *Subsection (7)* provides that before publishing the Framework he must consult any other persons or bodies as he thinks fit and obtain the consent of the Secretary of State. The Framework may be revised *(subsection (8))*.

### *Section 22: Co-operation and delegation*

129. *Subsection (1)* provides that any person or body with functions under any enactment of carrying out assessments of children's services must, for the purposes of those assessments, co-operate with other persons or bodies with such functions.

130. *Subsection (2)* enables a person or body with functions of carrying out assessments of children's services to delegate their functions to any other person or body with such functions.

### *Section 23: Sections 20 to 22: interpretation*

131. This section applies for the purposes of sections 20 to 22.

### *Section 24: Performance rating of social services*

132. This section amends section 79(2) of the Health and Social Care (Community Health and Standards) Act 2003 (c.43) (annual reviews). Section 79(2) of that Act requires the Commission for Social Care Inspection (CSCI) to review each local authority in England's social services provision annually and award the authority a performance rating. This amendment means that CSCI will award one performance rating in respect of services to children and care leavers (subsection (2)(a)) and another in respect of all other social services (subsection (2)(b)).

## Part 3 - Children's Services in Wales

## General

### *Section 25: Co-operation to improve well-being: Wales*

133. As in section 10 in relation to England, the purpose of this section is to create a statutory framework for local co-operation between local authorities in Wales, key partner agencies ("relevant partners") and other relevant bodies ("other bodies or partners"),

including the voluntary and community sectors, in order to improve the well-being of children in the area. The duty to make these arrangements is placed on local authorities and a duty to co-operate is placed on the partner agencies listed in *subsection (4)*.

134. *Subsection (1)* imposes the duty on each local authority to make arrangements to promote co-operation between the authority, its relevant partners (listed in *subsection (4)*) and other bodies exercising functions or engaged in activities relating to children in the local authority's area. The duty on each relevant partner to co-operate is in *subsection (5))*.

135. *Subsection (2)* sets out the purposes of the arrangements and *subsection (3)* requires a local authority, when making those arrangements, to have regard to the importance of parents and other persons caring for children in improving the well-being of children.

136. *Subsection (6)* gives a power for all the specified partners to pool budgets and other non-pecuniary resources in support of these arrangements. A pooled fund is defined at *subsection (7)*.

137. *Subsection (8)* creates a power for the Assembly to issue guidance on how these arrangements should work. The guidance will be used to explain the expected practical manifestations of co-operation between the core partners and wider relevant bodies, including the voluntary sector and users of services. These will include: effective working together to understand the needs of local children and young people, agreeing the contribution each agency should make to meet those needs, effective sharing of information at a strategic level, and integrated planning of services. The guidance will, in particular, make clear that there is no expectation that Children's Trusts will be created in Wales. *Subsection (9)* provides that the Assembly must obtain the consent of the Secretary of State before giving guidance under *subsection (8)* to non-devolved bodies.

### *Section 26: **Children and young people's plans: Wales***

138. This section creates a power for the Assembly, by regulations, to require children's services authorities in Wales to prepare and publish a single plan or a framework of plans for services to children and young people. This is intended to provide for greater coherence as to the precise obligation of children's services authorities and their partners and to give a statutory basis to the Children and Young People's Framework Partnerships and Children's Partnerships that are already in existence. It will rationalise their relationship with the Young People's Partnerships that already have a statutory basis under section 123 of the Learning and Skills Act 2000.

139. *Subsections (2) and (3)* set out the particular provisions which regulations under this section may make.

140. *Subsection* (4) provides for regulations to require the Assembly's approval of a children's services authority's plan and for the Assembly's modification of such before publication.

141. *Subsection* (5) requires a children's services authority to have regard to Assembly guidance in discharging its planning functions.

142. *Subsection (6)* provides a definition of 'relevant young persons'.

### *Section 27: **Responsibility for functions under** sections 25 **and** 26*

143. *Subsection (1)* of this section requires a local authority in Wales to appoint a lead director for children and young people's services with responsibility for co-ordinating and over-seeing the arrangements made under sections 25 and 26. This will not affect the existing service delivery responsibilities of the Chief Education Officer and the Director of Social Services. It is anticipated that an existing director, or even the chief executive, will usually be appointed as the 'lead director'. The lead director will ensure

that the partnership planning process is given a high profile within the local authority and acts as a driver for strategic planning for children and young people in the local authority area. At the elected member level his responsibilities will be matched by a 'lead member for children and young people's services'. As with the lead director, the lead member may also hold other responsibilities.

144. *Subsections (2)* and *(3)* require NHS trusts and Local Health Boards, as the local authorities' most significant statutory partners in providing services for children and young people, to appoint lead executive and non-executive directors (in the case of an NHS trust) and a lead officer and member (in the case of a Local Health Board) to deal with the arrangements under section 25. As with local authorities, these persons may also hold other responsibilities.

145. *Subsection (4)* provides for the Assembly to give guidance relating to this section. In practice, it is expected that this guidance will be integrated with that under section 25.

### *Section 28: **Arrangements to safeguard and promote welfare: Wales***

146. Reference should be made to the notes in respect of section 11, which makes the equivalent provision in respect of England. This section imposes a duty on specified bodies or persons to make arrangements to ensure that their functions are discharged having regard to the need to safeguard and promote the welfare of children. The aim of this duty is to:

- complement the general co-operation duty (section 25);
- ensure that agencies give appropriate priority to their responsibilities towards children;
- encourage agencies to share early concerns about safety and welfare of children and to ensure preventative action before a crisis develops.

147. *Subsection (1)* lists those bodies and persons to whom the section is to apply, and *subsection (2)* sets out the duty. The reference in *subsection (1)(h)* to services under section 123 of the Learning and Skills Act 2000 is to youth support services provided as part of the 'Extending Entitlement' initiative.

148. *Subsection (4)* provides that those persons and bodies mentioned shall have regard to guidance given to them by the Assembly. In the case of a police authority, a chief officer of police, a local probation board, a youth offending team or a secure establishment the guidance will not be issued by the Assembly but by the Secretary of State after consultation with the Assembly, as stated in *subsection (5)*.

### *Section 29: **Information databases: Wales***

149. The notes to section 12 apply, save that in Wales guidance will be given and directions issued by the Assembly. Regulations under this section may only be made with the consent of the Secretary of State.

### *Section 30: **Inspection of functions under this Part***

150. This section makes provision for the functions of a children's services authority in Wales to be subject to inspection by the Assembly.

### *Sections 31-34: **Local Safeguarding Children Boards: Wales***

151. The notes to sections 13 to 16 apply save that, in Wales, guidance to devolved bodies will be given by the Assembly. Guidance to non-devolved bodies will be given by the Assembly only with the consent of the Secretary of State. Regulations that make provision in relation to Board partners whose functions are not devolved to the Assembly may only be made with the consent of the Secretary of State.

## Part 4 – Advisory and Support Services for Family Proceedings

### CAFCASS functions in Wales

#### *Section 35: Functions of the Assembly relating to family proceedings*

152. This section confers on the Assembly the functions currently carried out for England and Wales by the Children and Family Court Advice and Support Service (CAFCASS). CAFCASS serves the Family Division of the High Court, county courts (including care centres), and family proceedings courts. The service safeguards and promotes the welfare of the children before courts dealing with family proceedings; gives advice to any court about any application made to it in such proceedings; makes provision for the children to be represented in such proceedings; and provides information, advice and other support for the children and their families.

153. The intention is that, following the coming into force of this section, responsibility for the welfare of children who are ordinarily resident in Wales who are or may be the subject of family proceedings as defined, will devolve to the Assembly. For all other children, responsibility will be retained by CAFCASS, although it is anticipated that there may be agreed reallocation of cases between CAFCASS officers and Welsh family proceedings officers, as defined in *subsection (4)*.

154. *Subsection (2)* provides that the Assembly must ensure that arrangements are made to enable Welsh family proceedings officers to exercise their duty as imposed by any enactment.

#### *Section 36: Ancillary powers of the Assembly*

155. *Subsection (1)* allows the Assembly to make arrangements with organisations to perform its functions under section 35. This would give the Assembly the option of contracting with some other body to perform the functions on its behalf. *Subsection (8)* makes it clear that such a body could be in the public, private, or voluntary sectors.

156. *Subsection (2)* allows any organisation doing this work to designate individuals to carry out functions of Welsh family proceedings officers.

157. *Subsection (3)* sets conditions of quality and value for money if the Assembly is to make arrangements with another organisation.

158. *Subsection (4)* enables the Assembly to make arrangements with individuals, such as self-employed practitioners, to carry out functions of Welsh family proceedings officers.

159. *Subsections (5) and (6)* allow the Assembly to second staff and provide services to those carrying out the functions, while *subsection (7)* allows it to charge for doing so.

#### *Section 37: Welsh family proceedings officers*

160. *Subsection (1)* provides that the Assembly may authorise a Welsh family proceedings officer to conduct litigation in relation to any proceedings in any court and to exercise a right of audience in any proceedings before any court, in the exercise of his functions as a Welsh family proceedings officer if he is of a description as prescribed by the Secretary of State.

161. By virtue of *subsections (2) and (3)* a Welsh family proceedings officer exercising a right to conduct litigation, or the right of audience under this section, is treated as having acquired that right solely by virtue of this section, and not by virtue of any qualification which he might have.

### *Section 38: Inspections*

162. This section allows the Assembly to request inspection and report on the relevant activities of the Assembly and Welsh family proceedings officers post devolution. Such a request will require the agreement of the Secretary of State as having responsibility for the inspectorate.

### *Section 39: Protection of children*

163. *Subsection (1)* applies the Protection of Children Act 1999 to the Assembly as though it were a childcare organisation for the purposes of the functions of the Assembly under this part. The Protection of Children Act relates to the suitability of people to work with children, and the section also provides for the Assembly to ensure that appropriate mechanisms are in place in any organisations carrying out the functions on the Assembly's behalf in order that the Assembly can be satisfied that persons employed by that organisation are suitable.

### *Section 40: Advisory and support services for family proceedings: supplementary*

164. The section brings Schedule 3 into effect.

### *Schedule 3 – Advisory and support services for family proceedings*

165. The amendments in *paragraphs 2 to 11 and 15 to 18* of the Schedule make provision relating to 'Welsh family proceedings officers' and their functions. In particular, the amendments confer the same functions on Welsh family proceedings officers as currently exist for officers of CAFCASS.

166. The amendment in *paragraph 13* limits the functions of CAFCASS to children other than those ordinarily resident in Wales.

167. The amendment in *paragraph 14* makes consequential provision relating to the membership of CAFCASS.

### *Section 41: Sharing of information*

168. This section provides for the Assembly and CAFCASS to be given powers for the mutual exchange of information where such information will clearly be in the interests of those children who are the subject of family proceedings and where it is in the interests of good practice and management issues. *Subsection (2)* provides for corresponding powers to be given to individual officers of both organisations.

## Transfers

### *Section 42: Transfer of property from CAFCASS to Assembly*

169. This section provides for a scheme agreed by the Secretary of State and Assembly to provide for the transfer of property, rights, and liabilities from CAFCASS to the Assembly.

### *Section 43: Transfer of staff from CAFCASS to Assembly*

170. The Secretary of State and the Assembly may make a scheme under this section for the transfer of employees from CAFCASS to the Assembly in order to enable the exercise of the new functions conferred on the Assembly. Under the scheme, the Assembly would inherit the responsibilities of CAFCASS as employer as though the original contract of employment had been with the Assembly and not with CAFCASS.

171. *Subsection (5)* provides that, should any employee object to transfer, then he is not to be transferred, his contract is terminated immediately before transfer and he is not to be

treated as though he had been dismissed. The section does not prevent an employee from ending his contract if a substantial detrimental change is made to working conditions.

172. *Subsection (7)* makes it a prerequisite to the making of a scheme for any prescribed requirement as to consultation with CAFCASS employees to have been complied with.

## Private fostering

### *Section 44: Amendments to notification scheme*

173. The law on private fostering arrangements and the role of local authorities with respect to them is set out in Part 9 of, and Schedule 8 to, the Children Act 1989 and in the Children (Private Arrangements for Fostering) Regulations 1991.

174. A privately fostered child is one who is under the age of 16 (under 18 if he is disabled) and who is cared for and accommodated by someone other than a parent, other person with parental responsibility or close relative. A child is not privately fostered if the person caring for them has done so for fewer than 28 days and does not intend to do so longer than that. There are a number of exemptions from this definition set out in Schedule 8 to the Children Act 1989.

175. The current legislative provisions relating to private fostering, referred to in these notes as the notification scheme, require those involved in a private fostering arrangement to give the local authority advance notice of it. Privately fostered children are not 'looked after' children in the terms of section 22 of the Children Act 1989 and local authorities do not get involved in the making of such arrangements, but they have to satisfy themselves that the welfare of privately fostered children in their area is satisfactorily safeguarded and promoted. They also have powers to impose requirements on arrangements and to prohibit them altogether.

176. The amendments in *subsections (2) to (5)* extend the duties of local authorities in cases where a child is proposed to be, but is not yet, privately fostered.

177. *Subsection (2)* amends section 67(1) of the Children Act 1989, under which local authorities are required to satisfy themselves that the welfare of privately fostered children is being satisfactorily safeguarded and promoted, so that the duty also applies in respect of children who are proposed to be privately fostered.

178. *Subsection (2)* also amends the duty on local authorities under section 67(1), which requires them to secure that such advice is given to those caring for privately fostered children as appears to the authorities to be needed. The amendment extends the duty to include advice to prospective foster carers and/or to parents. The intention is that local authorities should be able to give such advice, for example, where one proposed fostering arrangement has been prohibited by the local authority and no other is currently contemplated. The parents may need advice then on what alternative arrangements can be made for the care of their child.

179. Section 67(2) of the Children Act 1989 gives the Secretary of State the power to make regulations about visits by the local authority to privately fostered children and imposing requirements which are to be met by local authorities in carrying out their functions under section 67.

180. The new subsection (2A), inserted by section 44(3), provides that the regulations made under section 67(2)(b) may say what local authorities have to do when they are told that a child is going to be privately fostered. The intention is that these regulations will require local authorities to carry out proper checks on, and satisfy themselves of the suitability of, a proposed arrangement or exercise their powers to prohibit, or impose requirements on, the arrangement before the child is privately fostered.

181. *Subsection (4)* amends section 67(3) of the Children Act 1989. The existing reference in this section to a person authorised "to visit privately fostered children" was not very

apt for a case where he is, under this provision, inspecting premises for children who are proposed to be privately fostered.

182. *Subsection (5)* amends section 67(5) so that the current duties of a local authority where it is not satisfied that the welfare of a privately fostered child is being satisfactorily safeguarded or promoted will apply in the case of children who are proposed to be privately fostered.

183. New section 67(6), inserted by *subsection (6),* gives the Secretary of State the power to make regulations requiring local authorities to monitor the way in which they discharge their functions under Part 9 of the Children Act 1989. It is intended that such monitoring might include keeping a record of notifications received, monitoring compliance with timescales for visits and recording any prohibitions or requirements imposed along with reports of any visits and the outcomes of notifications. This information could then be collated in an annual report to Local Safeguarding Children Boards. The intention of this provision is to increase the focus of local authorities on private fostering.

184. *Subsection (7)* inserts a new paragraph 7A into Schedule 8 of the Children Act 1989. This will require local authorities to raise public awareness of the requirement to notify the local authority of private fostering arrangements.

185. *Subsection (8)* provides that the new regulation-making powers inserted into the Children Act 1989 by this section will, with respect to Wales, be exercised by the National Assembly for Wales.

### *Section 45: Power to establish registration scheme in England*

186. *Subsection (1)* gives the Secretary of State the power to set up through regulations a scheme for the registration of private foster carers. More detail of the scheme is provided in the rest of the section.

187. *Subsection (2)* provides for regulations to make supplementary provision relating to the registration of people for private fostering and sets out some matters in relation to which such provision can be made.

188. *Subsection (2)(a)* says that the regulations may make provision as to how a person applies for registration and as to the procedure to be followed by the authority in considering an application. It is supplemented by *subsection (3),* which highlights that the regulations may make it an offence for a person, in an application for registration as a private foster carer, knowingly to make a statement which is false or misleading in a material way.

189. *Subsection (2)(b),* which makes for provision in the regulations as to the requirements to be satisfied before a person may be registered, is supplemented by *subsection (4),* which sets out some detail of what these requirements might include. These are the requirements with which all prospective private foster carers will need to comply in order to be registered.

190. *Subsection (2)(c),* which concerns the circumstances in which a person is disqualified from being registered, is supplemented by *subsection (5),* which sets out in more detail the circumstances in which regulations may say that a person is disqualified. *Subsection (6)* allows the regulations to provide that the authority may determine whether a person is or is not disqualified. This means that even if someone might otherwise be disqualified the authority could decide that nevertheless they should be able to be registered.

191. *Subsection (2)(f),* which makes provision in the regulations as to the imposition by a local authority of conditions on registration and as to the variation or cancellation of conditions, is supplemented by *subsection (7),* which makes provision for what these conditions might include. These conditions are requirements imposed at the discretion of local authorities only on particular people. For example, a condition would be

appropriate where a local authority wanted a particular person to do something to become suitable for private fostering (e.g. does something to their premises).

192. *Subsection 2(j)* makes for provision in the regulations as to other requirements that might be imposed on local authorities or registered persons. It is supplemented by *subsection (8),* which makes provision for a requirement that a registered private foster carer obtain the consent of the authority before privately fostering a child so that the authority can check on the appropriateness of the arrangement for that particular child. If the authority is not satisfied with the arrangements for that child, then they may prevent the care of that child with that private foster carer. This will not affect the registered status of the private foster carer. *Subsection (8)* also makes provision relating to the giving of such consent by the authority.

193. In relation to *subsection 2(j), subsection (9)* makes provision for a requirement that authorities undertake annual inspections in relation to registered private foster carers (whether or not they are at the time privately fostering children) and for the payment of fees by registered persons in respect of such inspections.

194. *Subsections (10) to (13)* deal with offences. *Subsection (10)* makes provision for regulations which may authorise a local authority to issue a notice to any person whom they believe to be privately fostering a child in their area while unregistered; and which may provide that a person would be guilty of an offence if, without reasonable cause, he/she continued to privately foster a child when such a notice was in force.

195. *Subsection (11)* makes provision for regulations which may provide for the offence of breach of requirements without reasonable excuse.

196. *Subsection (12)* makes provision for regulations which may provide for an offence where a person who is disqualified from registration fosters a child privately, unless he is disqualified because he lives in the same household as someone who is disqualified or in a household in which such a person is employed and did not know and had no reasonable grounds for believing that the other person was disqualified. This offence carries a more severe penalty, including possible imprisonment, reflecting the greater seriousness of the offence.

197. There is no offence merely for breach of a condition imposed by the local authority. If there was breach of a condition, the local authority would have to de-register the person before any criminal offence could bite.

198. *Subsection (14)* will enable the repeal of those parts of the Children Act 1989 which will be incompatible with the registration scheme and to add functions under this provision to the functions listed in Schedule 1 of the Local Authority Social Services Act 1970 (making them social services functions).

### *Section 46: **Power to establish a registration scheme in Wales***

199. Section 46 confers the same power on the National Assembly for Wales as Section 45 confers on the Secretary of State.

### *Section 47: **Expiry of power in sections 45 and 46***

200. *Subsection (1)* provides that if no regulations have been made under section 45 within fours years of Royal Assent, that section will cease to have effect at that time.

201. *Subsection (2)* makes the same provision for Wales.

202. *Subsections (1)* and *(2)* operate independently, so if regulations are not made in England within the four year period, the power in section 45 expires even if regulations have been made under section 46 in Wales (and vice versa).

## *Section 48: Child minding and day care*

203. This section gives effect to Schedule 4.

## *Schedule 4: Child minding and day care*

204. This Schedule makes minor amendments to Schedule 9A of the Children Act 1989 which was introduced by the Care Standards Act 2000.

205. *Paragraph 2* enables conditions imposed by a court or tribunal upon a child minder or day care provider's registration to be treated in the same way as conditions imposed by the registration authority. This will clarify the status of conditions imposed by a court or tribunal and the enforcement action that may be taken by the registration authority if these conditions are breached.

206. *Paragraph 3* makes clear that fees for registration as a child minder or day care provider are payable on application for registration and are non-refundable.

207. *Paragraph 4* creates more flexibility in the way that the registration authority can levy ongoing fees by removing the requirement that fees be 'annual'.

208. *Paragraph 5.* Under Schedule 9A, a person may be disqualified for registration for child minding or day care. That has the result not only that the person may not be registered, but that he may not be concerned in certain ways with the provision of day care (paragraph 4(4) of the Schedule) or be employed in the provision of day care (paragraph 4(5)). However, disqualification may be waived (paragraph 4(3A)). The purpose of the amendment is to clarify that waiver of disqualification may be granted not only for registration itself but also for the purposes of the prohibitions in paragraphs 4(4) and 4(5).

209. *Paragraph 6* removes the requirement upon the registration authority to make an assessment as to whether all persons looking after children are suitable to do so, and all persons living or working on the day care premises are suitable to be in regular contact with children. As part of its determination as to whether the applicant is qualified for registration, the registration authority will check that the employer has appropriate procedures in place to make suitability assessments, thereby enabling him to qualify for registration. The registration authority will continue to assess the suitability of the person in charge of a day care setting and to assess that the applicant is qualified for registration under section 79F.

210. *Paragraph 7* provides that Part 10A of the Children Act 1989 does not apply to the provision of day care in a hotel (or other similar establishment) for children staying in that hotel where the day care is provided only between the hours of 6.00 p.m. and 2.00 a.m. and the person providing the day care (which could be the hotel or an agency) does so for no more than two different clients at the same time.

211. *Paragraph 8*. At present a person who is disqualified from registration for providing day care may not be concerned with the management of day care, or have any financial interest in the provision of day care. *Paragraph 7* removes the prohibition on disqualified persons having a financial interest in day care, and limits the scope of the prohibition relating to management to disqualified persons who are *directly* concerned with the management of day care.

212. *Paragraph 9* clarifies that unincorporated associations can be registered in their own name rather than in the name of individuals who make up a particular association. It ensures that enforcement action can be taken against the association as a whole as well as, where appropriate, against responsible individuals.

## *Section 49: Payments to foster parents*

213. This section relates to payments made to foster carers in England and Wales.

214. *Subsection (1)* enables an order to be made making provision for the level of payments to be made to foster parents caring for looked after children placed with them by local authorities (including those with whom children are placed through independent fostering agencies) and to foster parents caring for children placed with them by voluntary organisations. *Subsection (2)* provides for such an order to be made by the Secretary of State in relation to England and by the Assembly relation to Wales.

215. *Subsections (3) and (4)* amend the Children Act 1989 to ensure that the discretion given to local authorities and voluntary organisations to decide rates of payment to foster carers is subject to an order under this section.

216. *Subsection (4)* of section 66 provides that the first order by the Secretary of State making provision for payments to foster carers must be approved by resolution of both Houses of Parliament.

## Local authority services

### *Section 50: **Intervention***

217. This section allows the Secretary of State or National Assembly for Wales to intervene where local authorities are failing to discharge functions relating to children's services to an adequate standard. It does so by extending existing powers of intervention relating to education functions.

218. The section applies section 497A of the Education Act 1996 (power to secure proper performance of LEA's functions) to functions which are relevant functions for the purposes of the sections. The relevant functions are set out in *subsection (2)* and include social services functions relating to children, functions in relation to children leaving care and functions under sections 10 and 12 of the Act (sections 25 and 29 in relation to Wales).

219. The Secretary of State's power to give a direction under section 497A arises where he is satisfied that a local authority is failing in any respect to perform any relevant function of a local authority to an adequate standard (or at all). The same test will accordingly apply in relation to the power as extended by the section.

220. *Subsection (4)* makes clear that the ancillary provisions of sections 497AA and 497B apply where the power in section 497A is exercised pursuant to this section.

221. *Subsection (6)* ensures that, where a direction is given under section 497A in relation to education functions, it can also extend to the functions referred to in *subsection (2)* (so that it is not necessary to give two separate directions).

222. This section does not restrict the use of other powers of intervention.

### *Section 51: **Inspection of local education authorities***

223. This section amends section 38 of the Education Act 1997 (inspection of LEAs). At present Ofsted (in England) or Estyn (in Wales) may inspect functions relating to the provision of education by a local education authority for persons of compulsory school age or persons above or below that age who are registered as pupils at a school maintained by the authority.

224. This amendment allows Ofsted (in England) to review *any* local education authority function, with the exception in England of functions which fall within the Adult Learning Inspectorate's remit. By virtue of the amendment Estyn (in Wales) will be able to review any local education authority function *and* functions under sections 25 (co-operation to improve well-being: Wales) and 26 (children and young people's plans: Wales), so far as those functions relate to education, training or youth support services.

### *Section 52: Duty of local authorities to promote educational achievement*

225. This section amends section 22 of the Children Act 1989, which set out the general duties of a local authority in relation to each child whom it is looking after. There is a duty in subsection (3) to safeguard and promote the welfare of the child. This section inserts a new subsection (3A) which places a particular duty on the local authority to promote the child's educational achievement.

226. A looked after child is defined in section 22 as a child in care (i.e. under a care order) or a child provided with accommodation by the local authority in exercise of its social services functions. There is evidence that this group of children achieve significantly less well than their peers, and that this under-performance is due at least in part to a lack of effective support from local authorities as 'corporate parents' of these children.

227. The new duty will mean that local authorities will have to give particular attention to the educational implications of any decision about the welfare of any child they are looking after. That might be for instance the need to organise a suitable school placement at the same time as arranging a new care placement.

### *Section 53: Ascertaining children's wishes*

228. This section amends sections 17, 21 and 47 of the Children Act 1989, under which a local authority has a duty to safeguard and promote the welfare of children in need in their area by providing suitable services to those children. The amendment requires a local authority to ascertain any such child's wishes in relation to those services and to give those wishes due consideration before determining what (if any) services to provide. Guidance issued under section 7 Local Authority Social Services Act 1970 in relation to section 17 already places considerable emphasis on listening to children and taking account of their wishes. Section 53 gives statutory backing to that approach.

### *Section 54: Information about individual children*

229. This section amends section 83 of the Children Act 1989 by inserting a new subsection (4A). Section 83(4A) enables particulars required to be transmitted by local authorities and voluntary organisations under subsections (3) and (4) respectively, to include information that relates to and identifies individual children. The type of information transmitted under subsections (3) and (4) will include name, a unique pupil reference number, and postcode. The information transmitted will be used to fulfil the Secretary of State's functions in relation to children and young people. In particular information on individual children will be used by the Secretary of State for statistical analysis in order to inform and review policy about children and young people. It will also be used to ensure that local practitioners have all the relevant and accurate information they need to carry out their functions.

### *Section 55: Social services committees*

230. This section removes the requirement on local authorities in England and Wales not operating executive arrangements under the Local Government Act 2000, to establish a social services committee by repealing section 2 of the Local Authority Social Services Act 1970, and related provisions of that Act (*subsection (1)*). The requirement in England to have a director of children's services means that there can no longer be single 'social services committees'. All references in law to social service committees are therefore repealed. In addition, local authorities in England will no longer have social services departments. Therefore references to such departments are removed.

231. *Subsections (2)* to *(5)* make amendments to Schedule 1 to that Act, section 63(8)(a) of the Health Services and Public Health Act, paragraph 4(1) of Schedule 1 to the Local Government and Housing Act 1989 and section 102 of the Local Government Act 2000, which are consequential to this repeal.

### *Schedule 5: Repeals, part 4 social services committees and departments*

232. The amendments in this part of this Schedule make a number of repeals which are consequential on the removal of the requirement to have social services committees made in section 55. This requirement only applied to authorities in England and Wales not operating executive arrangements under the Local Government Act 2000.

233. Some other amendments in this part of this Schedule relate to the removal of anachronistic references to social services departments in existing legislation, but do not affect the meaning or effect of any of the Acts amended. The amendments have been made to avoid any potential ambiguity given the potential for authorities to split social services functions between two departments (children and adult).

## Other provisions

### *Section 57: Fees payable to members of independent review panel*

234. Section 57 amends section 12 of the Adoption and Children Act 2002 (c. 38) (independent review of determinations). Section 12 provides for the establishment of a review procedure in respect of qualifying determinations made by adoption agencies. This is intended to provide prospective adopters with a right to request a referral to a panel established by the appropriate Minister, where an adoption agency indicates that it is minded to turn down their application to adopt. Under subsection (4) of section 12 the appropriate Minister may delegate functions in relation to the panel to an organisation to perform on his behalf. Under subsection (3) of section 12, regulations may provide for the duties and powers of a review panel, its administration and procedures, appointment of panel members, payment of expenses, the duties of adoption agencies in connection with reviews and the monitoring of reviews.

235. Section 57 amends section 12(3)(d) (power to make provision as to the payment of expenses of members of a panel), by replacing the words 'expenses of' with 'fees to'. This will provide for regulations to be made to provide for the payment of fees to members of a panel constituted under section 12. This will help the organisation to which the appropriate Minister delegates his functions to recruit panel members and is consistent with provision in the Adoption and Children Act 2002 Act, which will allow adoption agencies to pay fees to their adoption panel members.

### *Section 58: Reasonable punishment*

236. Section 58 removes the defence of reasonable chastisement in any proceedings for an offence of assault occasioning actual bodily harm, unlawfully inflicting grievous bodily harm, causing grievous bodily harm with intent, or cruelty to a child. It also prevents the defence being relied upon in any civil proceedings where the harm caused amounted to actual bodily harm, which has the same meaning as it has for the purposes of section 47 of the Offences Against the Person Act 1861. The defence would still be available in proceedings before the Magistrates Court for common assault on a child.

237. The section removes the defence by providing that battery of a child cannot be justified as reasonable punishment. Battery is any unwanted application of force to the body of another and is more commonly called "assault". However it has long been recognised by the law that a parent or person with parental authority may use reasonable punishment to correct a child. This is the defence of reasonable chastisement or "reasonable punishment". Other defences to battery are not affected by section 58.

238. *Subsections (1) and (2)* remove the defence in relation to the offences mentioned above. The parent is thus in the same position as if he had assaulted an adult or a child over whom he exercised no parental role.

239. *Subsection (3)* removes the defence in civil proceedings for any battery if the battery caused actual bodily harm. *Subsection (4)* provides that 'actual bodily harm' in

*subsection (3)* has the same meaning as has been established in relation to criminal proceedings.

240. *Subsection (5)* repeals section 1(7) of the Children and Young Persons Act 1933 in consequence of *subsection (2)(c)*.

**Section 59: Power to give financial assistance**

241. This section amends section 14 of the Education Act 2002 (c. 32) to extend the powers of the Secretary of State (in relation to England) or the National Assembly for Wales (in relation to Wales) to give, or make arrangements for the giving of, financial assistance. *Subsections (2) and (3)* detail the purposes of the new powers: the promotion of welfare of children and their parents, and the provision of support for parenting. Children are defined for these purposes as under twenty. These new purposes add funding powers for children's services to the existing broad education funding powers. The effect (in relation to England) is to provide a statutory basis for giving financial assistance to activity across the new wider responsibilities of the Secretary of State for Education and Skills. These include responsibilities for children's services and parenting following the creation of the position of Minister for Children, Young People and Families.

***Section 60: Child safety orders***

242. This section extends the existing circumstances in section 8 of the Crime and Disorder Act 1998 in which courts can make parenting orders and amends the power to make child safety orders contained in sections 11-13 of the 1998 Act. At present, the only sanction for breach of a child safety order is a care order. That sanction is being removed by *subsection (4)*. Instead, we are creating (by *subsection (2)*) the possibility of the making of a parenting order.

243. Child safety orders can be made in a Family Proceedings Court when: a) a child below 10 has committed an act that would have been an offence were he 10 or over, b) imposing the order is necessary to prevent a child below 10 committing such an act, c) a child below 10 has contravened a ban imposed by a local child curfew scheme, or d) a child below 10 has behaved in a manner that caused or was likely to cause harassment, alarm or distress to one or more persons not of the same household as the child.

244. The order places the child under the supervision of a responsible officer from either a social services department or youth offending team, and requires the child to comply with specified requirements. The purpose of the requirements is to ensure the child receives appropriate care, protection, and support, is subject to proper control, and to prevent the repetition of the kind of behaviour which led to the order being made.

245. Courts may already make a parenting order under section 8 of the 1998 Act when they make a child safety order. *Subsection (2)* creates an additional circumstance in which a court can make a parenting order. This is when a court determines that a child has failed to comply with a requirement of a child safety order. The court will only be able to make a parenting order in this circumstance where it is desirable in the interests of preventing a repetition of the kind of behaviour which led to the child safety order being made. All other provisions currently relating to parenting orders made in the same proceedings as child safety orders under section 8(1)(a) of the 1998 Act will apply equally to these new parenting orders.

246. This new power allows a parenting order to be made at a later stage. It could be used when there were insufficient grounds to make a parenting order when the child safety order was made, for example, where it appeared that the parent had done everything he could to prevent the child misbehaving but it had since emerged that one would be desirable in the interests of preventing repetition of the behaviour which led to the child safety order being made. This may be because a parent is no longer co-operating, or that co-operation from a different parent or guardian is needed to secure the child's compliance in meeting the requirements of the child safety order.

247. Section 11(4) of the 1998 Act restricts the maximum duration of a child safety order to three months other than in exceptional circumstances. *Subsection (3)* extends the maximum duration to 12 months. This gives more time to address the child's problems and is also in line with the maximum duration of a parenting order, with which the child safety order is usually linked. By making the permitted duration the same, an order on a child can be supported by a matching order on the parent over the same period to address the behaviour of the child.

248. *Subsection (4)* removes from the court the power, when a child safety order is breached, to make a care order at a lower threshold than is required by section 31 of the Children Act 1989. This power had been seen as a barrier to the use of the child safety order. If the court believes that the parents, with appropriate support, could secure the child's compliance with the order, it could make a parenting order under *subsection (2)*. If a parenting order had already been made with requirements mirroring the child safety order's requirements, the court could fine or impose a community sentence on the parent for breach of the parenting order. If the court concluded that the child is beyond parental control it could, under section 37 of the Children Act 1989, direct the local authority to consider applying for a care order. The court would also retain its power to vary or discharge the order.

249. All other provisions relating to child safety orders under the 1998 Act will remain the same.

### *Section 61: Children's Commissioner for Wales: powers of entry*

250. Section 61 gives the Children's Commissioner for Wales the power to enter premises, other than private homes, to interview children when reviewing and monitoring the functions of and arrangements made by the Assembly and other specified persons. The power does not apply to the Commissioner in the discharge of his function of conducting examinations or considering and making representations on any matter, under sections 74 and 75A of the Care Standards Act 2000.

### *Section 62: Publication of material relating to legal proceedings*

251. Section 62(1) amends section 97 of the Children Act 1989 to make clear that the publication of material from family proceedings which is intended, or likely, to identify any child as being involved in such proceedings (or the address or school of such a child) is only prohibited in relation to publication of information to the public or any section of the public. This section will make the effect of section 97 less prohibitive by allowing disclosure of such information in certain circumstances. In effect, this means that passing on information identifying, or likely to identify, a child (his school or his address) as being involved in court proceedings to an individual or a number of individuals would not generally be a criminal offence.

252. It is envisaged that rules of court will set out the cases in which publication of information relating to children is authorised. Being authorised by rules of court, such publication will not constitute contempt. *Subsection (2)* amends section 12 of the Administration of the Justice Act 1960 to make it clear that the reference in subsection (4) to publication which does not constitute contempt includes cases where the publication is expressly authorised by rules of court.

253. The remaining subsections amend rule-making powers to enable the rules to be made.

### *Section 63: Disclosure of information by Inland Revenue*

254. Section 63 amends Schedule 5 of the Tax Credits Act 2002 to enable the Inland Revenue to share Tax Credit, Child Benefit or Guardian's Allowance information (except where it relates to a person's income) with local authorities (or, in Northern Ireland, Health and Social Services Boards) for the purposes of enquiries and investigations relating to the welfare of a child under the legislation specified in *subsection (2)*.

255. *Subsection (3)* enables those authorities to pass this information on to other people or bodies (e.g. the police) for the purpose of such enquiries or investigations without the consent of the Inland Revenue. It also enables authorities to pass information from the Revenue to others for the purposes of civil or criminal proceedings or where the Revenue would have had the legal power to do this themselves. However, *subsection (4)* provides that, in these circumstances, authorities are required to seek permission from the Revenue beforehand.

256. In any other cases, *subsection (5)* makes it an offence for a staff member of an authority to disclose information provided to him/her under *subsection (1)* unless the disclosure is made:

- in accordance with an enactment or order of court,
- with the consent of person to whom the information relates, or
- in a way that prevents identification of the person to whom the information relates.

257. This places a criminal sanction against unauthorised disclosure by the authority's staff, which reflects the existing Inland Revenue criminal sanction against unauthorised disclosure of information by Revenue staff. *Subsection (6)* provides that a person charged with this offence has the defence that he/she reasonably believed that his/her disclosure was lawful. In practice this means that the onus of proof is on the defendant. If found guilty, *subsection (7)* would mean that a person is liable to a maximum of two years imprisonment.

258. Section 67(7)(k) provides that s*ection 63* took effect on the day on which the Children Act 2004 received Royal Assent.

### *Section 67: Commencement*

259. Part 1, which establishes the Children's Commissioner, section 59, the power to give financial assistance, and section 63, which allows disclosure of information by the Inland Revenue will come into force on Royal Assent.

260. Sections 45 to 47, which create the power to establish by regulations a registration scheme for private foster carers in England and Wales, section 49 which creates the power by order to make provision on payments to foster carers, and section 58 which restricts the use of the defence of reasonable chastisement, will come into force two months after Royal Assent.

261. The rest of the Act's provisions will be brought into force on dates appointed by the Secretary of State or, where specified, by the National Assembly for Wales by commencement order. In particular:

- Sections 25 and 31 will be commenced by the National Assembly for Wales except where their provisions relate to non-devolved bodies in which case they may only be commenced with the consent of the Secretary of State.
- Section 28 will be commenced by the National Assembly for Wales insofar as its provisions relate to devolved bodies. Provisions relating to non-devolved bodies will be commenced by the Secretary of State after consulting the National Assembly for Wales.

## Hansard References

262. The following table sets out the dates and Hansard references for each stage of this Act's passage through Parliament.

| ***Stage*** | ***Date*** | ***Hansard Reference*** |
|---|---|---|
| ***House of Lords*** | | |

*These notes refer to the Children Act 2004 (c.31) which received Royal Assent on 15th November 2004*

| ***Stage*** | ***Date*** | ***Hansard Reference*** |
|---|---|---|
| Introduction | 3 March 2004 | Vol. 658 Cols. 657-8 |
| Second Reading | 30 March 2004 | Vol. 659 Cols. 1208-310 |
| Committee | 4 May 2004 | Vol. 660 Cols. 1036-96 |
| | 6 May 2004 | Vol. 660 Cols. 1218-57, 1273-344 |
| | 20 May 2004 | Vol. 661 Cols. 878-914, 925-1000 |
| | 24 May 2004 | Vol. 661 Cols. 1052-124, 1137-86 |
| | 27 May 2004 | Vol. 661 Cols. 1441-88, 1507-24 |
| Report | 17 June 2004 | Vol. 662 Cols. 870-902, 922-1004 |
| | 21 June 2004 | Vol. 662 Cols. 1013-30, 1043-76 |
| | 22 June 2004 | Vol. 662 Cols. 1208-34 |
| | 5 July 2004 | Vol. 663 Cols. 518-603 |
| Third Reading | 15 July 2004 | Vol. 663 Cols. 1414-97 |
| ***House of Commons*** | | |
| Introduction | 19 July 2004 | Bill 144 2003/4 |
| Second Reading | 13 Sept 2004 | Vol. 424 Cols. 1000-88 |
| Committee | 12 Oct 2004, 14 Oct 2004, 19 Oct 2004 and 21 Oct 2004 | Hansard Standing Committee B |
| Report and Third Reading | 2 Nov 2004 | Vol. 426 Cols. 173-281 |
| **Lords Consideration of Commons Amendments** | 10 Nov 2004 | Vol. 666 Cols. 993-1008 |

| | |
|---|---|
| **Royal Assent**— 15 November 2004 | House of Lords Hansard Vol. 666, Col. 1185 |
| | House of Commons Hansard Vol. 426, Col. 1009 |

Adapted and published by GRANGIS under the OGL Licence 3.0.

www.nationalarchives.gov.uk/doc/open-government-licence/version/3/

GRANGIS - UK PUBLISHING 2022.

www.ingramcontent.com/pod-product-compliance
Lightning Source LLC
LaVergne TN
LVHW060214210926
848481LV00008B/2740